D1728166

20/20
A Poetic Diary Of A Historic Year

Volume I

By
Mary Alexandra Stiefvater

BOOKS BY MARY ALEXANDRA STIEFVATER

POETRY
Cocoa For Saturdays
On The Merry-Go-Round
The May Project
Love East Of The Sun
From Grace
Unknown Beauty
Poems From Alta California
Somewhere East Of Eden
Valkyrie
Autumn Son
Of The Americas: West
Of The Americas: East
Time And The Artist
What Grief Stole
20/20 (Volumes I, II, III)

PHOTOGRAPHY
In My Contrary Garden
Fair The Rose
The Sun She Sets
La Vie En Rouge
Wild & Domestic
Lux
Near & Away
Skyscape

20/20

A Poetic Diary Of A Historic Year

Volume I

By
Mary Alexandra Stiefvater

20/20 (Volume I, II, III)

31st Republic Productions
www.31strepublicproductions.com

This book is dedicated to

All the healthcare professionals
who stood on the frontline protecting us

Thank you

TABLE OF CONTENTS

MARCH

APRIL

AUTHOR'S NOTE

Thank you for joining me on this journey! It is my
sincere hope you enjoy this book as much as I
enjoyed writing it.

Punctuation and line breaks are funny things.
They can substantially change a piece. They can
make a poem more or less meaningful to the
reader. I invite you to try reading these pieces
differently each time and sharing them with
someone you love.

Also, I invite you to change the pronouns to fit
your needs within these works. Poetry belongs to
all of us and should feel inclusive. Where possible
I have strived to use various pronouns to reflect
our varied world. The use of the "I" pronoun in
this book reflects, not the author, but rather an
invitation to the reader to the see yourself in the
work.

And finally, there are some sensitive topics within
this book. This was a heavy and dark year for all
of us and some poems may be difficult to read.

Stay safe. We'll be together again one day soon.

PREFACE

Back in 2014, I started an experiment. I decided to try and write a poem a day for an entire month. The result turned into *The May Project*. But what if I could expand the experiment? Could I write a poem a day for a year? Hmmm...

I thought why not try. It couldn't hurt. Little did I know what 2020 would hold...
At first it was a bit of a slog. The poems were short. But by a month into it, I noticed the poems were finding me. I was writing multiple poems a day. This was definitely not expected. The more I practiced, the easier it became. I noticed the work changed depending on the time of the day I wrote, what happened in the news cycle and my daily struggles.

Then somewhere in the middle of the first quarter, COVID-19 took over our lives and subsequently this experiment.

So much happened while we were in various stages of lockdown or reopening. We watched the world from our windows, unsure of what life would look like afterwards. We had no idea how many people this virus would take or how grief would be delayed due to necessity to survive. We held our breaths, but not each other. And more questions came than answers...

This was a historic year that changed us

irrevocably. Its effects on our lives will be felt for
generations to come.

What follows is a diary of 2020.

A poem a day. For one year.

January

<u>I WISH</u>

I wish I wrote like Walter Benton
Indelibly inking myself into your blood
Or Alfred, Lord Tennyson
Slipping into your bosom
Syllable by gentle syllable
Perhaps Angelou
Bending words to shape
The curl of your sweet mouth
I wish, like Emily Dickinson
I could fit your beauty, my desire
Into a stanza
Or the palm of your tender hand
Revealing my naked soul, fumbling at your spirit
If I was but Yeats
I could warm your body
By the fire of my poem
Just lusty enough to convey
But elegant so as not to offend
Oh, that it was Carol Ann Duffy's words
Not mine, that filled our wide night
As the room and our bodies turned
Shall I remind your sacred ear
That I am not Langston Hughes, John Donne,
Walter Benton
I wish
I wish
I wish I was
But still I would change nothing of you
Were I Pygmalion
...Or perhaps God

JANUARY 1

THE PENDULUM

The pendulum
Is on the move again
Swing back in opposite time
Crossing the threshold of middle
To bring us to another place
Another direction
Another something we are not prepared for
Even though we've been there before
And the mercurial point
To this madness
Is still a mystery
As we still across the table
Facing our foe
Who looks strangely like ourself
Back and forth
The momentum grows
Pushing us further away from middle ground
Further from our comfort
But somehow back to where
We have already been

JANUARY 2

NEW YEAR

Open the door and
Throw out the dead flowers
A wide world is
                    Waiting

JANUARY 3

EPIPHANY

Presents for the first
A tree to last the twelve days
The King is forever

JANUARY 4

LONELY, ALONE

It's hard to be lonely
Alone
Shadow puppets
Use to be fun
Cake for birthday breakfast
A love note in school lunches
A hug at bedtime
It's hard to be lonely
Alone
Now I mend my coat
Sigh folding the laundry
There's no cake in bed
And I make my lunches now
It's hard to be lonely
Alone
Without love notes, shadow puppets
Hugs and you
It's lonely
Without you

JANUARY 5

A COUPLET

Brother, O Sister, we come and go and pass
without
But today, I see you and we meet as friends

JANUARY 6

AS YOU KNEEL

Do you really have to
Ask her the question
You know the answer

JANUARY 7

A WASTED DAY'S EFFORTS

I must write a poem
Write a poem
I must write a
Damn! I have nothing
To write
About, today
Does this happen to
Others, stuck, blank on a page
With nothing to show
For the effort
Stop, just stay calm
You will write a poem today
A poem
A poem
Oh damn!
Nothing.

JANUARY 8

A TALL HEART

They say height matters
When it comes to the heart
So he waited for a tall one
Not short and sweet
Not flat and reclined
Not even normal
Tall for tall
Or none at all
He waited patient
For his heart to come
Tall for tall
Not lovely and small
He waited
And waited
Resigned this heart
Would not arrive
Slumped in bed
Sadly
But the double doors
Blew open anon
"She's here," someone yelled
Your tall heart
She's here for you
He cried grateful
She found him
And after a bit
As he reclined
He felt her tall heart
Skip a normal, lovely
Sweet beat
In his chest

And he felt tall again

JANUARY 9

THE COAT

Did you know that day you bought it
As you slipping your arms on through
That one day your daughter would wear it
As she does, she'll think of you?

Did you sense as you picked the color
That blue would match her eyes?
Did you know that day you bought it
That you'd both fit the very same size?

Did you put your hands in the pockets
The same now she does too
Thinking this coat will keep her stylish
Just like it does for you?

Did you pick the woolen model
For its length that she will don
Knowing one day it would be there
To hug her when you're gone?

Did you know when you bought it
That one day we'd be here
Me on a winter morning
Wrapped in love from ear to ear?

JANUARY 10

FAILING AT ADULTING

Was it always this hard?
Or is it just me?
No really!
Can you keep up?
I can't...
The news, the dishes
The climate, the traffic
Was it always this hard
Or did we just make it worse?
And the failure crushes
What's left of our hope
As rents increase
Home prices rise
Medical cost bury
And education debt
Is a life-long sentence
Was it always this hard
Being an adult
Or is it just me?
As one more child
Shouts to a parent
I can't wait to be a grown up!
Life will be so much better!
No really...
It was always this hard!
I just didn't know it then
Because the adults who parented me
Were so good
At making it look easy

JANUARY 11

THE ESSENCE LEAVES

The essence leaves
Once the heart stops
Swinging the face
Into a contortion
The proverbial "Ah"
And the wrinkles smooth
The skin tightens
The hair loses its smell
The essence leaves
Once the heart stops
A quick departure
Pulling away the pain
As if it never existed
And suddenly it doesn't
Look like her anymore
As the bones lay silent
Trapping her secrets forever
No longer can I see her
In that face
She is somewhere in the ether
The essence, matter around me
Now
I know I had no right
To keep her
Now she is free
Still...my heart is broken

JANUARY 12

SHOES

Shoes in the bathroom
Shoes down the hall
A shoe in the doorway
That is really quite small

A shoe in the sofa
Shoes underneath
The table, the dresser
Even where they both sleep

Shoes for a Monday
Shoes for the night
For every occasion
Shoes that fit right

Shoes in the bathroom
The kitchen, the stairs
But she likes to go barefoot
So still, they'll lie there

JANUARY 13

IF

The pencil to the page
Scratching like a needle to vinyl
Longing to find its melody
In composition
Alas, it feels more like mortar to brick
Upon beginning
Sticking to the page
When it longs to sing
But a pencil can build a house
Win a Grammy
Sketch a masterpiece
In words or lines
If it tries
IF...
But it relies
Upon the choice
To pick it up
Courageously and begin

JANUARY 14

BILL

Selling you a bill
To get the job
Making bills
That represent
Them & theirs
That gave up bills
To get their name
On a ticket
To sell you a bill

JANUARY 15

<u>UNCIVIL</u>

Like a hurricane
They blow in
Causing destruction
With their chaos
Consuming all the air
And attention
In the space
And a silent groan
Takes shape
In the eyes
Of the inhabitants
Whose quiet
Afternoon is disrupted
By this group
Of nobodies
Pretending to be somebodies
Loudly

JANUARY 16

THEREFORE I WRITE

Were I but William
Blake, before the tiger, God
I would be a poet

JANUARY 17

SMALL VICTORIES

The sale of a book
The glance of a certain someone
Your voice raise above a crowd
Command of the room
Seeing a new version
Of the same person you stare at in the mirror
Tying a shoelace
Breaking a barrier
Buying a house
A car
That first edition you have hunted for forever

Small victories indeed

JANUARY 18

I LOVE YOUR BODY

I love your body
It houses you
Said the Lover
Inside it, your wit
Your heart, I couldn't love it more
Your smarts, your essence
Every shape and line perfection
Every curve and bend, an alter
I love your body
It houses you

                          No! She screams
                Declaring the mirror truth
                           See this here?
                             Fat! And this...
                     A distortion of self!
                   This spot and that scar
              Render me unlovable, Lover!
                     Leave this sad mass
        Of skin and cells and disappointment
                   Find another...better...
                               Please...

Are you done?

                                      No!

              It has been starved and stretched
                    Corseted and covered
          The flavor consumed, then spit out
                Stuffed into jeans too tight

                              Sweaters too loose
                         And lingerie too hateful
                          And still it is not right
                      Not true, not worthy of you

Stop, whispers the Lover
Turning her chin from the mirror
Begging
See your truth
In my hands
Your essence reflected in my eyes
I love your body
It houses you

Feel these hips
Your journey is written in them
Your feet speak of purpose
Written long ago in the stars
Those fingertips hold memories
Of lives before
And lessons learned
And your back
The cornerstone
That with your spine
Your lovely spine
Holds up this vessel
I so dearly adore

                                                    No!

Yes!

Believe me when I say

I love your body
It houses you…
Your sharpness and glass
Your raw and metal
Your cement and earth
I could not love a house more
Because you are in it!

Do not lock me out
Leaving me to cry on your porch
I found my home
In a vast and wide universe
So please believe me
When I say
I love your body
It houses you

JANUARY 19

ALL THE SOFT BITS

All the soft bits
Like retriever puppies
And dandelions
Sunshine on your naked shoulder
Soft
The worn flannel shirt
I stole from your closet
The place
Where your ankle and calf join
Soft
A midnight kiss
Under a mountain of feather down
The water droplets on your neck
All those bits
Soft
The vulnerable reach of your hand
When you don't know my answer
The almond blossoms in the breeze
Your whisper that stops the fear
All the soft bits
That I love

JANUARY 20

SAID GRAMPA

Don't get old, he said
It isn't very fun

> But Grampa, why?

They stare when you
Try to stand
They try to take
Your projects away
They won't leave you be
Fussing and fighting you
To do what you've done
All along
Don't get old, he said
Your skin gets wrinkled
And blotchy
You fall asleep in the day
They don't let you dance at parties
And sometimes you forget how to play

> But Grampa...
> I like your polka dotted hands
> And I like walking slowly with you
> I like how we sit on the sofa
> Talking an hour or two

> They get nervous
> When I try to cross
> The street
> They take all my projects away
> They tell me to eat all my vegetables

They don't listen to what is say
It doesn't seem very different
Whether you are very old or young
Someone is always barking orders at you
Someone is trying
To take all your fun

Let's go get some ice cream!

But don't tell them!

JANUARY 21

TONIGHT

Collapsed in a heap
Of disappointment
Not always good
Sometimes perfunctory

JANUARY 22

TENDERLY

Tenderly he comes
To rape the trust
Right out of him
He wants
What he wants
So he takes it, tenderly
Convincing himself
That this is right
This is love
This is what
The night smells like

                              And though
                        He does not want it
                          Did not ask for it
                         Could not stop it
                      Even though it's tender
                          Still he is raped
                         Still he is shocked
                          Still he will hide
                          This somewhere
                         In a dusty corner
                             Of his mind
                         Next to the time he
                      Learned to ski and skate
                      Tucked deep in the folds
                             Of the mind
                        And the bed sheets

               Stuffing it somewhere
               That muffles the screams

That dulls the shock
As tenderly
He is raped
Unable to stop it
Unable to trust
He will ever be
Loved again

JANUARY 23

CROONER

There's a cricket crooning to me
Singing a torch song, Romeo in my bathroom fan

JANUARY 24

SNOWED

The hours bleed
Into weeks, months
What should help doesn't
And snowed, he is buried
Under the avalanche
Of blankets
Of cocktails
Of SSRIs
Of disappointment
And depression
They swore it would work
But
All there is
Is darkness, sleep
But not death
This is not life
Snowed
Held in this suspended place
Barely breathing
Unable to move
Unable to live
But not dead
And the mountain
Seems unbearable
Buried under blankets
Under cocktails
Under despair
And lost times

JANUARY 25

THE FORK

The fork scratches across the plate
Looking for substance
But it is never lifted
Just left to scratch the bone china
Pushing vegetables
And lean protein
In a circular manner
Making dinner art
How the fork longs to serve
To be lifted
But she won't do it
Measuring the self-hatred
By how much she can leave
On the delicate pattern
That belonged to her grandmother
Until finally the fork is reclined
Because she has found
Another excuse
Not to eat

JANUARY 26

SOMEONE'S DAUGHTER

All the money in the world
Can't buy back that moment
Can't take away that pain
All the money in the world
Can't stop the advance
Can't make him sleep sound
All the money in the world
Can't levy back her power
Can't stop his hands
All the money in the world
Can't amplify her NO
Can't muffle his YES
All the money in the world
Can't give her back her lost self
Can't buy back her innocence
And all the money in the world
Will never be enough
To reclaim what was stolen in Colorado

JANUARY 27

COMFORT THE POET

Comfort the poet
Lull the child
A dark wind is blowing
Dig in, hold tight

Soothe the adult
Who is loose at the string
A wild night is coming
Dig in, hold tight

Hug the musician
Grace be the artist
Comfort the poet
Dig in, hold tight

A dark wind is blowing
Time and tide is high now
Lull this here child
Dig in, hold tight

JANUARY 28

CAN WE BE MERMAIDS AGAIN

Does a tree weep
When a person sits on its roots?

Do jellyfish fear
Peanut butter and bread?

Do summer skies get jealous
Of autumn's colors?

Does gelato dream of being ice cream
And ice cream, of being a cone?

Are zebras smarter than we think?
Do reindeers hate pink?

How will our mothers find us
When we die?

Were we once mermaids
Before we walked on land?

Can we be mermaids again?

JANUARY 29

HOMERO

The pool of water
Drenched your wings
As your delicate body
Lay softy at the bottom
A well near the southern home
You died protecting good
The black of their crime
The orange of your aura
You, El Monarcha
And they, assassins of a king
So the butterflies weep

JANUARY 30

OUR MODERN SAINTS

Dear St. Baller,
Make me great
Make me rich
Help me get the girl/boy

Dear St. Tech Entrepreneur,
Make me great
Make me rich
Help me get the boy/girl

Dear St. Movie Star,
Make me great
Make me rich
Help me get the girl/boy

Dear St. Socialite,
Make me great
Make me rich
Help me get the boy/girl

Dear St. Politician,
Make me great
Make me rich
Help me get everything

Let's canonize another
...For the hell of it

Dear St. Social Media,
Make me great
Make me rich

Help me be ~~loved~~ liked

Amen

JANUARY 31

February

INTO THE NEBULOUS

Into the nebulous
The brightest star at our center
Fading
As we hold tight to the ether
The matter in-between
Clinging to
The part of ourselves
We still remember
A void in
The brain matter
A black hole
Unknown
As we hurdle towards
The unstoppable
Into the nebulous
Our bright star dying

FEBRUARY 1

THE POISON CAKE

Love, like cake
Each bite irresistible
The first taste, an introduction
To the intoxicating sweetness
That follows
Each bite tantalizing
You need more
But heartbreak...a poison
Vomiting love out
Of your body
Worse than eating sand
The taste of it in your mouth
Making you heave and retch
Falling to your knees
You lay on the floor
Begging
For it to end
Heartbreak is that poison
Conceded in the cake
And if it doesn't kill you
And if you survive it
Cake is the last thing
You'll ever want

FEBRUARY 2

MR. HERNANDEZ

There's a trail of dead butterflies
Lining the southern path
Activists and monarchs
Confronting a gruesome task
They are slain
And lying wingless
Robbed of their very flight
There's a trail
Of death
It's time
For all to fight

FEBRUARY 3

FEBRUARY IN LA

The zealots pass out
Their apocalyptic flyers
Begging us to repent
The somebody
Who is nobody
Honks his horn
In a hurry to get nowhere
The worker bees
Jump on and off the bus
Walking with purpose
So no one bothers them
It's February
In Los Angeles
Windy, cold
The jasmine blooming
At night
We are already imagining
Summer's breath
Hot upon our cheeks
The sun drops orange
Over the ocean
Creating a cityhenge
Between skyscrapers
We wonder where
Our dreams went
Somewhere between
Rent, 2 jobs and a side hustle
The zealots are wrong
The apocalypse has come
And gone
And we are still here

Hustling
Trying to keep the faith

FEBRUARY 4

OF JUSTICE

Heel strike too loud
Someone driving in the wrong gear
A brokedown Porsche
The pencil with a sassy message
Daffodils un-bloomed
Blue coat, warm day
Mismatched couple
Life repeating
A poem stuck
In the mouth of a poet
Dogwood trees
Dead butterflies
Activists slain by cartels
An un-impeachment
Justice miscarried
A judgement from both sides
The two-headed quarter
An unremarkable day
Non-organic toilet paper
Bamboo overgrown and unruly
Love these sassy pencils
A heel strike too loud
Driving in the wrong gear
A brokedown Porsche
Slain activist
Un-impeachment
A miscarriage
Of justice

FEBRUARY 5

LIBRARY

The uncirculated air
A stale reminder
Of the sins
These walls have seen
Transgressions
But the dust isn't talking
The rug still dented
From where
The heavy
Masculine club chair sits
The curtains smell
Of cigars and wood cleaner
A library of disgust
The books know
The desk knows
The shawl carelessly hanging
Off the piano knows
Fortunately for her
They pretend they don't
And she can avoid
That room

FEBRUARY 6

NO. 35

Can you hear the people
Sing? Shout? Demand
Their voice be counted?
Be heard?
A doctor died today
And dissent fell upon
This scorched earth
As we stayed up all night
Praying
Praying
Praying for him
Until prayers were no longer enough
Crafting a song of unity
That reverberated from the trees
From the wet market
From the web
From a hospital
Where a doctor died today
Can you hear the people?
Sing! Shout! Demand
Their voices be heard!

This is what revolution sounds like

FEBRUARY 7

US QUESTIONING

The woman on Maple
Selling her wares on street racks
Instead of the boutique dreamed of

The muralist, in her kitchen
Afraid of her ex-husband
And herself

The procrastinating poet
So afraid of failure
He may never write that book

The filmmaker who draws the blinds
Unable many days
To leave the house

The teacher who wonders
What life would have been like
If they had listened to their mother

The short man whose complex
Will cause domestic violence
And his co-workers know it

The genius janitor
Who is cleaning an office building
He is intelligent enough to own

The uncompromising zealot
Whose epiphany
Is suddenly causing consternation

The middle schooler
Who doesn't understand
Why the world and her parents are backwards

The black Labrador
Licking his owners hand
Wondering how to get a biscuit

The gumball machine
Who stands desperate
For some fresh candy and a thorough cleaning

Us questioning
Our faith, our politics, our cages
Wondering if we can break free

FEBRUARY 8

OUR PARKS, THEIR HOMES

Bears ears
A moose nose
Deer antlers
Mice toes

Ferns and moss
Redwood trees
Aspens quivering
Honey bees

Monarchs floating
Trout swim by
Chipmunks squirreling
Mother Nature sighs

Pleading with us
Protect their homes
From Bears Ears, Zion
To Yellowstone

FEBRUARY 9

WHERE DID JOY GO

Is she hiding under the bed
Wrapped in wrinkled sheets?
Did I mislay her somewhere
Leaving her to fend for herself?
Where did Joy go?
There was a time
I bounded out of bed
Eagerly dressed and fed myself
Caffeine was not my drug
She was
Where did Joy go?

I did not dread the week
I did not scrap by
I did not hide in plain sight
Invisible
She lit me up
And I sparkled
Where did Joy go?
Did I put her in the pocket of a coat
Sent to the cleaners?
Is she hiding in a box
At the bottom of my garage?
Did I lend her to a friend
Who never gave her back?
Where did Joy go?

I'm sorry
I let you down
Grew up, changed
I'm sorry my bones got lazy

And my heart got broken
Too many times
I'm sorry I didn't
Let you help me mend it
Let you find the spring
That lifts me from my bed
Let you dress me
In the love I deserve
I'm sorry Joy

Won't you please come back?

FEBRUARY 10

PLUM TREES

You have another life under your skin
As if you belonged to another time
And place
As if we knew each other before
When samurai swords were sharp
And we could hold a grain of rice
On our earlobes
We would lay under the window
Watching the moon drench the plum trees
In silver light
When your only possession was a comb
And you gave it to me
A time and place no longer
As we sit on opal cliffs
Drinking wine and watching surfers
Get drenched by waves of blue
Tangled in seaweed
You were someone else once
And I remember it
Every time I look at you
As you put the comb
In my long, black hair
I watch the
Plum trees in the moonlight

FEBRUARY 11

~For JC~

I AM NOT A POET

I am trying to write you
A love poem
But I am not a poet
You give chase
To something in me
Something I cannot catch
And as your light bends the corner
Calling me to you
I have no words
I only have
The memory of this love
That never happened

FEBRUARY 12

WHEN LOVE WAS STILL ETCHED

When this new love was still etched
Upon our skin
When we ate raw cookie dough
Oblivious to the consequences
When acne and the dance
Were our two biggest problems
When silk was too fancy to wear
And cotton fell loose upon us
When we were drunk on youth
Afloat on that 12 AM kiss
When movies stars still had an allure
An unknown mystery
But we were the ones
That stood on pedestals
Every Friday night
When we still sleep soundly
The entire night long
When we couldn't wait
For what we did not know
When work was balanced
Between play and fun and play
When we made hearts with butter knives
In the peanut butter jar
When we were worried about our future
But only until three o'clock
When everything but adults made sense
And we were the smart ones

But piggy banks break
Dreams fall into muddy puddles
And summer crushes fade away

Still there was a moment
A time wrapped in blankets
And hot cocoa
When everything made sense
When this new love was still etched
Upon our skin

FEBRUARY 13

THE POINT

You try and you fail
You try and you fail
You try and you fail
And you fail
And you fail
And you fail
And you fail
But still you try
And that is the point
You keep trying

FEBRUARY 14

POOL

Childhood seems enchanted
Only once you've left it
But while you are in it
It feels like a long, slow burn
That you are dying to escape
Only to leave it
And wish you were there again
Instead of sitting in a waiting room
Waiting for a surgery to end
       Dreaming of those summers spent
       In your sister's friend's pool
       Playing mermaid
       For hours and hours
       Fingers pruned
       Smelling of chlorine
       Hair a bit greenish
       Your mother doesn't make you bathe
       You spent so much time already
       In the water
       Free and happy
       Peeling off your swimsuit
       You hang it in the shower
       Put on your jammies
       And sleep
That's all you want to do is sleep
But the doctor comes out
To tell you that...
       And there you are
       A mermaid again
       Drowning
       At the bottom of a pool

FEBRUARY 15

BLOOMS UNSEEN

I was going to see
The almond blossoms today
Alas, I had work

FEBRUARY 16

MICROCLIMATES

It's stormy in the living room
Fog predicted in the shower
The back bedroom is sunny and warm
But the kitchen has a bomb cyclone brewing
The doghouse is hazy with a chance of a biscuit
Everyone dispersed
To the corner of their sphere
To ride out their microclimate
Quick someone order pizza
Or else the dining room
Might become a hurricane

FEBRUARY 17

SATIATE

In this love, you feed
Feasting on my tender heart
But I, satiate

FEBRUARY 18

ABANDONMENT

You scream
You yell
You self-destruct
Taking me with you
I leave
Unwilling to take it
You beg
You plead
You cajole
I return
Convinced you have changed
Are sorry

You scream
You yell
You self-destruct
Taking me with you
I leave
Unwilling to take it
You beg
You plead
You cajole
I return
Convinced you have changed
Are sorry

You scream
You yell
You self-destruct
Taking me with you
I leave

Unwilling to take it
You beg
You plead
You cajole
I return
Convinced you have changed
Are sorry

You scream
You yell
You self-destruct
Taking me with you
I leave
Unwilling to take it
You beg
You plead
You cajole
I do not return
Convinced I deserved better
Than this abuse
You are vindicated
"See", you say
"Everyone leaves me!"

FEBRUARY 19

TO DO

Busy day
Much to do
What can I say
Must get through

Busy day
Go to, go to
So anon I leave
To do, to do

FEBRUARY 20

WHAT MAKES A FRIEND

He wondered one day
Scrolling through sent photos
Of "friends"
Would he be in them
Counted as close
If not for poverty's disparity
Would he be the host
The invitee, the honored guest
If they were aware
Of how hard he tried
If the cards or calls
Were considered enough
True tokens of friendship
Of caring
That showed his devotion
Not trips
Or presents
Or hosted events
If not for economics and ignorance
Would all those people have stayed close
Seen him
Valued his contribution
His friendship
However humble
Would he be in the photos too
Loved
And supported
Despite poverty's disparity
He wondered
What makes a friend
The kindness one could afford?

Or money spent?

FEBRUARY 21

OWED A POEM

I owe myself a poem today
Did my duty
Worked hard
And now it's night
And as I cozy and warm sit
I remember
I owe myself a poem
Not too long
Not too short
Just enough to be
Enough
After work and errands
Something lovely
To cozy up to
So I wrote this

FEBRUARY 22

THE WORLD TURNING

The faces change but
Love, joy and reasons to thrive
Persist, we are human

FEBRUARY 23

GOODNIGHT SWEET

A Barcalounger
Mickey D's
The funeral heard round the world
Purple led lights
New boots
Margaritas on a Sunday
Happy hour without the happy
Scripts
Celebrities
A virus
Santa Anas
Avocados
Tomorrow...will never come
Tomorrow...too fast is
Here we are
Namaste
A time capsule
Synchronicity
Cannes, Cannes
Can do it
Rinse and repeat
Social media is overwhelming
Overrated
Not social today
Time flies
Catch it in your palm
Funeral
Funerals
Emails gone astray
Time, more
Time

Goodnight sweet
Prince

FEBRUARY 24

FOUND

Found
A wish
Lying in a gutter
Flat and bruised
But still a wish
A little worse
For wear of years
Somewhat tarnished
But still a wish
It was from a time
Before I was born
Scratched and forgotten
But still a wish
So I lifted it
And smiled a bit
As I pocketed
And gave home to
This my new wish

FEBRUARY 25

BY

Life is passing
By holidays
That celebrate
Whether you
Do or not
By seasons
That bloom
And change
And frost
Whether you
Watch or not
By kids
That grow
And become adults
Whether you
Are a parent or not
By death
As it is
Part of the cycle
Of rebirth
And renewal
Whether you are
Ready or not
Life is passing
By

FEBRUARY 26

WHO HMONG US

We are the mothers
That crossed the river
With children on our backs
We are the guardians
Of democracy, of freedom
Protecting ideals on foreign soil
We are the travelers
Who wrote our climb
On bruised thighs
And broken bones
We are the pilgrims
Brought to safety
From the danger
Across a river
Across an ocean
We are the Americans
Now deserted
As policies, laws and whims change
We are the mothers
Who carried our children
To the safety you promised
Who Hmong you
Will stand up for us?

FEBRUARY 27

LA TREES

Kaffirboom coral
Jacarandas blooming spring
On an LA day

FEBRUARY 28

A LEAP DAY SENRYŪ

I don't, I don't, I
Don't have poem today, so
I wrote this instead

FEBRUARY 29

March

THE PRICE OF FAME

The whiskey stings
There is no freedom in this wealth
In this glamour
The ringing never ceases
And the comments don't either
She is a ghost
In her own life
And she fears the likes
The comments
The hearts
And emoticons that rise
Because the hate rises too
The anger
The judgment
And she can't take it anymore
The whiskey stings
But everything else is numb
And the loneliness
The loneliness
The aloneness
 Is too much...

MARCH 1

THE COST OF DREAMS

Worn from the dream
She wore on her heart for years
Everything she wanted
And yet the joy
Was not there
Layers of something
But
Not what she thought she wanted
Frail after all these years
Spent
From the cost of her dreams
Is this the price
Of ours?

MARCH 2

ALONE FOREVER BUT TRUTH TOGETHER

The struggle to be yourself
The struggle to stay healthy
The struggle to raise a child
Alone

The struggle to get the job
The struggle to keep your home
The struggle to stay young
Forever

The struggle to stay
The struggle to go
The struggle to know
Truth

The struggle to heal
The struggle to love
The struggle to live
Together

MARCH 3

THE MARKET

The market highs
The market lows
The global parent
That controls our house
Tells us how to
Vote, Spend
Live, Love
Buy, Sell
And we listen
Not always actively
But still we listen
As this parent
Runs the house
And all the dreams
It does not sanction
We must leave behind
We go screaming
Like toddlers in a fit
But this parent knows best
And so we oblige
So there is always
A roof
Milk
Dinner
A bed
Safety
The market always wins
As long as we live in its house

MARCH 4

A BED OF STARS

Of lust and chaos
A marriage of kinetic and potential
Cooled and condensed
        Into a secret
A trail of broken stardust
Somewhere between the d-star hexaquarks and
Faith
Galaxies far away
We must have been whole once
Conceived in a bed of stars
Because what can't be seen is most abundant
And we are bountiful in this love
The kind of science that matters
Pondered by astronomers and poets
For eons and light years
A love explainable
Only by watching the reaction
Of the universe around us

MARCH 5

SITTING STILL

So overwhelmed
So angry
So tired
Eat more?
Sleep less?
No time left
To cram in more work
Ever enough?
Ever enough!
Ever enough...
As the body collapses
On the step
Slumped in exhaustion
Staring into oblivion
Just sitting
Found just sitting
Sitting still
Doing nothing
But sitting
And the heart starts to slow
The anger releases
The face relaxes
Sitting
Could the antidote
Be as simple
As nothingness
Practiced daily
Sitting still?

MARCH 6

A LONDON COUPLET

I miss the promise of a life
That existed twenty years ago

MARCH 7

WHITE CLOUDS

White clouds on the horizon
But grey clouds overhead
Another woman was beaten today
For standing
For her rights
In a world where she hasn't the right
White clouds on the horizon
But grey clouds overhead
Numbering in the billions
Here we stand
One day Maria
We will win
One day Jasmine, Rashida, Song, Zahra and Catori
One day
White clouds on the horizon
But grey clouds overhead
And my grandmothers
Clouds themselves now
Weep
At how many of us it took
Just to get to this moment
And how many more
Jasmines, Rashidas, Marias and Songs will wait
One fist in the sky
One cradling
The child at her breast
Before
Equality is our name
White clouds on the horizon
But grey clouds overhead

MARCH 8

~ For International Women's Day ~

IT KEEPS SCRATCHING AT THE BRAIN

Clawing recklessly
The record that keeps repeating
Over and over
It can't settle
Or quiet itself
It keeps tying itself up
As it tries to unravel
Scratching
Scratching
Clawing at the brain
Close your eyes
And it just gets louder
Never the good stuff
That's not what replays
Late in the night
It's the other
The loud and painful other
The unsolved problem
The unkind comment
The family squabble
The life choices questioned
Scratch, scratch, scratch
Repeating recklessly
As you try to reason
With the unreasonable mind

MARCH 9

HOLDING ONTO A FRAGMENT

Holding onto a fragment
Of what we knew
And that has changed
The world has shifted
Moved in a direction
We did not expect
And as we stand lost, unsure
We are darker, heavier deeper

MARCH 10

FLATTEN THE CURVE

Bend it, push it, stretch
It flat, as the curve panics
But we will survive

MARCH 11

MARCH OF SPRING

The air smells green
Of earth and irises
Crocuses and tulips
The wind tastes of spring
With hope
Wafting through the window
And joy
Sliding herself
Under the door

MARCH 12

PANDEMIC

The curve that hasn't bent
The shelves that are bare
The panic that isn't soothed
The worry
Terror
Fear

MARCH 13

WE, THE HUNTERS

March blew in
Like a lion
Like a pandemic
And instead of going out
To smell the flowers
We locked ourselves
Away, holed up
Crying
As it spread from West to East
Our greatest fear spread with it
And the panic
That sits in our hearts
Keeps us awake
Makes us feel
Like nothing will ever be
The same again
And it won't
But we've survived worse
And however long it takes
The lion, that is,
Will not defeat us
For We, the hunters
Shall not be hunted
We, the people
Shall not be defeated

MARCH 14

WINGS

She laugh when I said
I'm sewing wings on my back
That's poetic
You should write that
They wouldn't believe me
But it's true
I sewed wings on my back
Today
Because I'm so desperate
To fly away

MARCH 15

EXOPLANET

She is staring at the vase
The one she has always hated
Children scream from the other room
As she wipes the food off dirty plates
The dog is drooling on the clean floor
She watches the sun shift to clouds
Out the window above the sink
The cacophony of noise
Moves through the house
And to the back
She walks into the hallway
The door ajar, beckoning
And all she can think about
Is running
Out of it and far away
Breaking that awful vase
In her departure
Meanwhile
Somewhere else in the universe
Iron rain is falling
Ripping a planet to shredded
Destroying the very ground it falls upon
Leaving death and debris
In its path
Her feet start to twinge
Desperate to take flight
Her fingers dying
To break something loudly
The noise crescendoing
In her head
As the open door

And the iron rain call to her

MARCH 16

TAKE FLIGHT

Only trapped if you choose
Kept and held
Only if you let yourself be
You decide which side
Of those gilded bars
You sit behind
Happiness is not a bird
It is the wind
That beckons the bold
Lifting their wings
If they are brave enough
To just
Jump

MARCH 17

STRANGE TIMES

We write
We sleep
We eat
We dance
We work
We clean
We sleep
We eat
We dance
We work
We write
We sing
We worry
We worry
We work
We eat
We eat
We worry
We eat
We sleep
We rise
We sing
We dance
We work
We wait
We worry
We worry
Oh damn
We worry

MARCH 18

THE MOOD OF ABUSE

I'm fine
It's fine
We're fine
Nothing to see
Nothing to say
Everything is fine

10 years
20 years
50 years

I'm not fine!
It wasn't fine!
We definitely weren't fine!
Why didn't anyone see it?
Why didn't anyone say something?
Will I ever be fine again?

YES!

MARCH 19

WHAT WE BUILT TOGETHER

Kids are hiding under tables
And behind curtains
Sticky fingers mark the hiding place
Hands carry bowls of love
To the table
And we dress the ice cream
With a chocolate coat
And sprinkles of fun
There is a mess all over
The checkerboard cloth
And you smile
After the cold rush passes
We travelled so far
To get to this full table
And as empty bowls
Get left in the sink
I marvel at
You
And what we built together

MARCH 20

AND THE EARTH HEALED

The humans were stilled
Stopped
And sent home

And in that space
Porpoises danced in the waters
Swans stretched their wings
And their necks
The water was so clear
The fish could finally see
What the humans had built above
The clouds fluffed themselves
Taking more width in the blue
Because there was no smoke
To stand in their way
The rivers ran colder
Faster, and the bears came out
Of hiding, to see what they had missed
The grass had a chance to recover
From being trampled on
The flowers took
All the time they wanted
To bloom under the sun
Birdsong filled the stillness
And crickets chimed in

When the humans were stilled
The earth healed

MARCH 21

GIRL IN A BOOK

I wish I was
The girl in a book
The heroine
Who gets it right
In the end
The one who figures it out
Who becomes
Who wins love
Outside the book
It's far more complex
Writing lessons
That are longer than a chapter
Some that can't fit
Into the binding
I am not the ugly ducking
Or the busy know-it-all
Not the tomboy writer
Or the lovelorn heiress
I am not the heroine
Of a book or life
I wish I was
Instead
I simple am
And my happy ending won't fit
Between two covers

MARCH 22

THE LONG GOODBYE

The long goodbye
Was short
Tempered by
Traffic patterns
And weather conditions
By car bingo
And new tomorrows
The long goodbye
Was too short by far
And barely enough time
To say how much
I love you
So I wrote you this

Goodbye my friend
Live big!

MARCH 23

ONE DAY

One day
We'll be fine
Be free
Be happy again
One day
We'll look back
On all we've learned
On what we accomplished
Together

...One day

MARCH 24

THE AFTERMATH

After the tires roll
And the dust settles
After the boxes are collapsed
And the dishes washed
Then returned to the cupboard
After the tears and depression
Then the restless night
And the long sleep
The aftermath
Has a sticky taste
Makes the muscles stiff
Hurts
And the only remedy
Is time

MARCH 25

SHADOW

The shadow follows
Pursuing
Haunting softly
Inconspicuous
But omnipresent
Lingering around a corner
Under a crevasse
Just under foot
Waiting for a moment
When relaxed
To sidle up
And murder joy within

MARCH 26

OLD ENOUGH

Old enough to get the joke
Still young enough to enjoy it
And all those others pass and go
With never a thought upon it
Finally all the age and wisdom
Collect into a moment
When youth and beauty blossom full
And there's knowledge enough to own it

MARCH 27

IN A WEAK MOMENT

Alright...go on
Teach me to love again
I dare you
If you must
Fight the hard to win battle
Just to lose
To time and abuse
And those unworthy
Who came before
But you seem cocky
Confident, sure
And I am too weary
To fight your wrong impulse
To warn you
Of the danger
So...go on...
Give it your best shot
And I'll just sit here
Unamused
As you ignore the
Damage, destruction
Loss
That led me
To sit down here
Try to erase
The silvery sighs
Left dripping off the
Moon drenched bed
Rewrite me
The aqua color of those eyes
That first stared

Into my soul
Sing a new song
Into these ears
To cover the poetry
Someone once called this body
And try to unbreak
All that came before
Go on...
I dare you

MARCH 28

ARTISTS UNDER ISOLATION

The musician paces the alley
While the ballerina, en pointe,
Is doing dishes
The poet vacuums
The actor sits staring
                              At the emptiness
The sculptor is still in bed
The painter uses the brush
                              To tie up her hair
All are alone with their thoughts
Quarantining their creativity
With their fear
Inside their bodies
Unable to use art
To release their isolation

MARCH 29

A POEM FOR TODAY

Today is weird
Boring
Sleepy
But also filled
With unexpected
Love
Surprises merely a text
An email
A call away
And it turns a corner
The day was something
Then became something better
And that is the lesson
I suppose
You never know
What today will hold

MARCH 30

ELEGY FOR SOMEONE I KNEW

Gone long, time
Was once our friend but
I blinked and you were gone
Long time ago when we were young
Plotting our takeover
Of the world
Before we knew its losses and abuse
We dreamed in pink and feathers
Chased foreign lives
And mounting victories
Nothing
Nothing
Nothing was impossible
Not even willing the lottery
How tender were we then

But death and taxes are constant
The crack of the whip
Across a naïve heart
Can change a direction
Can change a course
And as the storm sets in
And the open wounds became scar tissue
I forgot
To look back
Pushing further into a changing life
A hard world
My demons clawing at these limbs
Pulling me under
Pulling
Pulling

Pulling me down
Until there was nothing
Not even dust
To lay upon

Then and only then I realized you died
Then and only then I realized I forgot
To check on you
Then and only then did I question
Why?
Why?
Why were we here?
I had left you
Forgotten
To die
As I journey forth
Pushed on
Fell down
Down
Down
And no matter how hard I tried
I could not remember you
Or us
Or the pink and feathers, dreams and victories
Lives we once though worthy to live
And as I lay there
With nothing not even you
I asked if I could go too
Gone?
Be gone?
Please...

No...

Push on...
Pull up...
There is something
Someone
You still need to meet

The knees knocked
The joints popped
The eyes swollen, face sallow
Emptiness all around
I climbed out of the grave
And as I neared the sun
There you were
Reaching for my hand
Pulling me up

You've met yourself
In all your incarnations
Let die the old versions
Just to continue the journey
You've been so many people
And no...you can't go back
But like a phoenix
You are always still becoming
And with each death
You will rise again

MARCH 31

April

ALL THE THINGS I DIDN'T KNOW

Will I
Ever see your face again?
Touch the softness of your cheek?
Raise a glass with you?
All the things I didn't know
I missed

APRIL 1

LOREN

His rosy cheeks
The bright, beautiful, brown of his eyes
The lips that held eternity
He loved her once
God knows why
But she was unworthy
Not worth his time
Or the poems he slid under her door
Or the accompanied walks
To lessons made every morning
She was not worth
This bright, beautiful man
And so they parted
But she never forgot
The kindness that was
Loren

APRIL 2

ALL THE PLACES WE GO

Curl up in those places
Where wounds heal
The cracks in the foundation
       The curve of his neck
       The small of their back
       The pillowy part of her stomach
       Her breast
       His breast
       Their breast
       A lap
Curl into the safety of a place
Where demons can't reach
Where the mind clears
       The curve of their neck
       The small of her back
       The pillowy part of his stomach
       His breast
       Their breast
       Her breast
       A lap
Held in those places
Safe
After this year
It's all the places
We long to go

APRIL 3

BLEEDING DAYS

The days bleed
Time, an open vein
Dripping seconds, minutes, hours
On the floor
As the Saturday
Never gets out of bed
And the Sunday
Became Tuesday
With just a nap
The hot bath
Makes it move faster
Pulling the moments
From you
And washing all of it down the drain
Leaving the body
Lying in the empty tub
Wondering what happened

APRIL 4

WILL WE EVER TOUCH AGAIN

Leave
Exit your home
You are free
Free again
But
When we see each other
Will we touch?
Can we hug?
Can we kiss?
Can we be us again?
Can we cross past the fear
Now that we know
What we know?
What we can't erase?
Because the world is different
And all I've been dreaming of
Is you
But you are different
I am different
The world we know is different
And I hesitate to do what is
                                   Natural
It looks like you do too...
Will we ever touch again
Without fear?

APRIL 5

GO BACK TO BED

Don't.
No!
Don't even think about it
Getting out of bed that is...Stop!!
Slide your feet back
Under the covers
Roll yourself up
Into a ball of blankets and sheets
Nope...Not even for a cup of coffee
Don't!
Just fall back asleep
And when you wake
It will all have been
Just a bad dream

APRIL 6

ORIGIN STORY

I do not come
For just your light
For all the brighter sides
Of your loveliness
I do not come for just your
Shooting stars
Milky way
Endless realms of chaos and glory
It's your dark matter
The secrets and sadness
Housed within
The stuff unseen
That composes you
Writing your personal anthem
Creating your potential
And whatever origin story
Wrote your dark matter
Made your light visible to me
And you unite my universe
In abundance

APRIL 7

TO ALL THE WOMEN DENIED

To the generations
Of women
Denied the right
To become yourself
To be an artist
Because a father, husband, society told you NO

     Your work was still seen

Recognized for the domestic skills and covert
ways
     You brought your talents to the world
The nightly suppers
     Birthday cakes
          Handmade cards
     Carved doorstops
          Homemade Christmas stockings
     The pillows and pillowcases
          Quilts
And your children know your artist's hand
In paper mâché volcanos
     Sewn Barbie clothes
          Photo ornaments on a tree
Millions of models of California missions
Built from whatever could be found in the garage
     Knitted sweaters
          Painted wall murals
     The brown bag lunch poem
          Made-up bedtime lullabies

     You were always an artist to your children,

to the children down the block, to the other
women who knew how much time and effort your
art took, to me

Your unabashed and selfless expressions fostered
generations, legions more

      And despite a father, husband, societal NO
      Thank God you kept creating
          For all of us, your fans

APRIL 8

SAID THE AUTHOR TO THEIR BOOK

The crack of the spine
The first flip
Of the virgin pages
Fresh with the smell of ink
The slick gloss of the jacket
This is what joy feels like
In tangible form
And every time I hold one
In these hands
For the first time
And each time I open one
Running my fingers
Down the binding
I know my purpose

APRIL 9

APRIL 10 ~ HOME SWEET HOME

A humming fridge and
A wall heater make sad company
In isolation

APRIL 10

<u>APRIL 11 ~ A COUPLET FOR THE FAITHFUL</u>

Still are we the devoted
If our doubt interrogates faith

                                        ?

APRIL 11

DO THEY PRAY FOR ME

Pray for them, my mother said
Passing on the way to school
Their work is tough
Their lives are hard
Pray God will see them through

And so the stigma
Of charity
Began with just one prayer
Of pity, poor and ugly
From a backseat as we stare

And years after
The smirks and tittering
The jokes and pointed hands
I wondered do they pray for us
In the damn near righteous land

For we are just as broken
Rough and aged
In saddened years
As those that deal in comforts
For a time distilling tears

Do you think they pray for us?
Do you think they would mind?
For I am stumbling even now
My own warrant
I have signed

The road that twists

And mires down
That changes path and course
Lands us sometimes honestly
On the backseat of a horse

That gallops far
From our good start
That forces adaption
Sometimes survival hinges on
The charity of one's own nation

And in this time of darkness
As the zealots wring their hands
I ask the lost
To pray for me
Because, I too am one that's damned

APRIL 12

FALSE SECURITY

Lulled into a sense
Safety with a mask on or
Scarf, but we're not

APRIL 13

SAKURA

Do the cherry trees still bloom
       If we are not there to see them?
       Inside staring at the window
           Do the delicate pink waterfalls
           Cascade down lonely trunks?

Somewhere near a power plant
       She stands
       Right where she has always stood
           For 1000 years
               Does she still bloom
                   In years of sorrow?
       When no one comes to visit...to say hello
       To see her wear the season
       A gown of petals, her perfume circulating
           Will she still put on her best
               If we are locked at home?

I hope so
It's nice to think
       Beauty goes on without us
       For one day we won't be here
           And Takizakura will still blush
            When the spring wind
               Whispers in her ear

APRIL 14

SUNNY SUN

I miss the sun
My legs and elbows
Shoulders, earlobes
Feel its absence
And no amount of rest at home
Can make-up a lost day
When the sun came out to play
But I was stuck inside

APRIL 15

KEEP SMILING

Behind the mask
They are smiling
As you pass in the parking lot
From a safe distance

Behind the mask
They are smiling
As you pick up your mail
Carefully

Behind the mask
They are smiling
As you share a joke
Through the drive-thru window

All around you
They are smiling
Even though
You cannot see it

Behind the mask
They are crying
As you exit the hospital
Alive

Stay safe world!

APRIL 16

THE STATE OF UNREST

The state that he wakes up in
The unrest that she always feels
The anxiety lurking eerily
The truth to be revealed

He makes it through his day
She stumbles to her home
They climb into their separate beds
Each one of them alone

They toss and they cannot sleep
They lie there wide awake
If only they were together
That is all that it would take

APRIL 17

A MAD COUPLET

All I have are expletives
And tears. That is the world today.

APRIL 18

WHAT IS LEFT AFTER YOU ARE NOT

You added shadow to my light
Bending the wholesomeness
Into something sinister
Supplementing happiness for pleasure
But never fully offering it
You contoured my lines
Evolving my totality
Into something totally different
Painting a new road
Through a tunnel
I never saw before you
Swallowing up me to become us
A molecule of chaos was all it took
To make me into something
Raw and opaque
No longer fresh and transparent
I was now a concoction of both of us
All of your melancholy
My bile
And the damaged sanguine of this love
Too damaged for either of us
And the remnants of the light left
Only serves to illuminate
The dark reaches
Just visible to anyone who bothers to look
Hard enough
I miss the light you took from me

APRIL 19

BOTH OF WHICH SCREAM

The days are silent
Except for all those damn birds
And tall hose damn thoughts

APRIL 20

SECOND WAVE

Still no guarantee
That it won't come again worse
So we wait at home

APRIL 21

OUTSIDE IN

Sometimes the extrovert
Goes inside
And never comes out
To play again
Staring through
A window, in
Their mind, locking
The door shut
That is where
The newly minted introvert
Learns
How to breathe again

APRIL 22

TIME CHANGES ALL

Wild the wind that blows
Changing the fortunes of time
While changing yours too

APRIL 23

<u>KEPT</u>

Some want more than anything
      To be kept
Some can't stand the confinement
      And freedom's price
      Is worth what they pay
      What they give up
So the barter continues and
Those kept
Embrace tightly, smiling
The notions of safety, security
Are the gold
Kept under their mattresses
      But those unkept know
      And are happier to remain
      Wild
      Their fortunes riding the wind
      Their notions, their own

          Just as they like it

APRIL 24

LOVE CANNOT ALWAYS OVERCOME GROWTH

Was it the snake
That sullied your heart
Forced the bite
Beckoned you to lie
Under that tree
Our tree
In the center of our universe

                    Or was it me?

The stars shone
The petals opened
The earth breathed
For us
But it wasn't enough
So I wonder, my darling

                    Was it me?

Just not enough
So you looked for the door
Out of paradise
Wonderful is only wonderful
If it's balance
Was our love not?

                    ...Don't answer that.

I forgive you, my Dearest
You were born too good
Too different
From me
And we could not mend that divide

But I shall always
Remember...
The fragment of our heaven
And the moment we first became
One, my Love

APRIL 25

FORWARD INTO SOMETHING

White knuckling the steering wheel
Trying to hold on
So as not to spin out of control
Control your breathing
In, out, in, out
Focus your eyes on the road
Stop crying
And as you round the bend
He stands out there
Waving as you pass
And it takes all that is in you
Not to turn around
Not to drive home
Not to ever leave again
But you are not only *that*
That cannot contain you
It's not your destiny
So you grip that steering wheel
Honk the horn and
Keep driving
Forward...into...something
Something yet to reveal itself
To you
To them
Remembering parting is not sweet
But the sorrow is necessary
If you are ever to own
You

APRIL 26

ARDOR

There is something primal
In the way she wants they
Something base
And every time she glance towards
The primeval ardor surfaces
Shaking the blood
Disrupting the conscious mind
Quickening the heart
She is ashamed
Wishing to be
More of the mind than the body
Elevating the discussion above
But something
Something
Something elemental happens
Every time she meets their eye

APRIL 27

REENTRY

Out of a warm embrace
With tears that seem endless
And heavy hands
Not from the baggage you carry
But the sadness of letting go
You hug again
One more time
Before you get into that taxi
On that airplane
Board that train
And it was...so good you didn't want to leave
Remembering how their body feels
What their hair smells like
How safe and happy it felt
To be held close
But you cannot stall any longer
And tears won't stop a departure
There is a life separate
To be lived
So you go
And as you are alone again
It feels jarring
The air is colder
The faces unrecognizable
Your body on autopilot
Your mind fighting reentry
And before you know it you are back
Back...in your own life
Your own city
Your own home
Alone

Feeling like an alien in your own world

APRIL 28

IN RESPONSE TO VIRGINIA WOOLF REGARDING ART

I have disappeared a long time
Finally returning
Anon.
Having dashed my ambitions
Suppressed the poet
Left remarkable sleeping on a pillowcase
But alas
Being back home
I still feel the old calling
Dreams still bursting at the seams
Writers of yore calling my name
From someplace unseen
The moors or the highways perhaps
Crazed, still with intent
To finish the work I love
And in this rightful night
I will leave the blossoms to rest
The dishes to soak
The tug of all those demanding
My attention, turned
To a purpose
My purpose
My reason and rhyme
Collecting it all on
A scrap, the back of the grocery list
A mirror
My hand
Leaving what was temporarily contained
Out in the wide open
Where it should be

APRIL 29

FIGS

He plucks the ripeness off the lone tree
Carrying in the buckets
And to the chagrin of the others
Dumps them on the table
Strays rolling off and onto the floor
Overtaking the kitchen
At least for the afternoon
The stewpot and cheesecloth come out
And the purple flesh gets washed
Then thrown into the pot
The white cotton veil hangs over the edge
Making a bed for the figs
I bite one and they are so ready the red seeds
explode
Out of the dark purple into my mouth
And they are so big I cannot eat them in one bite
He stirs them with the wooden spoon
The one long enough to reach the bottom
And then out them come
The white cloth now stained
As they are laid across the screens
To sun bake for days
We check the racks rotating this summer fruit
Until they are a fraction of what they were
Shriveled and small
But even sweeter
We sample, checking
That they are ready for the others
Knowing full well they are perfect
And the other come running
As the racks are brought in and bagged

Each doing their own quality control
Each having the same thought
...Perfect
And the lone tree
That gave up its harvest
Bent and silly looking in the backyard
Smiles
As we gobble down the fruits of its labor

APRIL 30

EPILOGUE

In the next 100 years there may be another pandemic. If this book remains, I hope it serves as a glimpse back in time to how we handled SARS CoV-2 (COVID-19); emotionally, socially, physically and spiritually. Life is always changing. The constancy of change and how we adapt to it will define us.

I hope history will remember all we attempted to do to carry each other forward into a brighter tomorrow.

ACKNOWLEDGMENTS

To Steve Stiefvater, Jonathan Singer, Nanci Roth,
Ian Springer, Kristina Lloyd, Courtney Logan
Krankall, Alysha Brady, Laura Napoli, Tamara Lelie
Skinner, who have championed my work,
corrected typos, read rough drafts and told me to
keep writing, in spite of the self-doubt.

&

With much gratitude to you dear Reader...
thank you for sharing your time and your heart
with me on this writing adventure. May we meet
again in the pages soon.

ABOUT THE AUTHOR

Mary Alexandra Stiefvater began writing poetry and studying photography from a young age. A native Californian, she was born in Chico and grew up in Stockton, later attending the prestigious School of Theater, Film and Television at the University of California Los Angeles. During her time at UCLA, Mary Alexandra spent a year abroad studying French cinema and philosophy at L'Université Sorbonne Nouvelle - Paris III and Le Centre Parisien d'Études Critiques. Upon graduation, she relocated to England to do her post-graduate studies at the London Academy of Music and Dramatic Art before moving to New York. Mary Alexandra resides in Los Angeles and in addition to being a poet and photographer, she is also an actor, model, award-winning screenwriter and filmmaker.

MARYALEXANDRA.COM

To see more from this author, please visit

MaryAlexandra.com
instagram.com/mary.stiefvater
Twitter.com/marystiefvater

&

To see more from this publisher, please visit

31stRepublicProductions.com
instagram.com/31st_Republic